10 Real Estate Investing Tips from Experts

How to Become Financially Free

Table of Contents

Introduction

Congratulations on downloading your personal copy of *10 Real Estate Investing Tips from Experts*. Thank you for doing so.

Real estate investing is probably the oldest form of investing, having been a part of human civilization since the beginning. The term real estate investing is a broad spectrum of financial activities, operating, and investing around making money through properties or a cash flow that is tied to the property.

Within real estate investing, you have four different ways to make money. Real estate appreciation is when an investment property increases in value. Cash flow income, which is a fancy term for rent, is when you make money through rental properties like apartment buildings, office space, or rental houses. Real estate related income is made by brokers and other specialists through buying and selling commissions. Ancillary real estate investment income comes from things such as vending machines or laundry facilities in apartment buildings.

There are so many different types of investments that you could consider for your portfolio. To make things easier, you should think in terms of major categories where investments could fall based on drawbacks and benefits, rent cycles and economic characteristics, property type, and customary lease terms. To help you make the best choices in real estate investing, the following pages will cover ten different tips to improve your investment strategy.

There are plenty of books on this subject on the market, thanks again for choosing this one! Every effort was made to ensure it is full of as much useful information as possible. Please enjoy!

Tip #1: Look at Your Resources

Real estate investing is really only a way to help your finances, so before you start diving into the detail of real estate, you need to look at your overall financial standing. Just like any journey, you have to first figure out where you are starting. With the journey of real estate, that means you need to review your resources honestly.

Pretty much all investors are looking to reach financial freedom. This can be seen as the top of the mountain where all of your living expenses are being covered by what you make from your investments. The fundamentals of getting to the top of the mountain will be the same no matter what you're investing in. To get to the top faster, you have to increase your savings rate. Those savings can then be invested in your chose asset.

We will look at ways to help your savings a little later on, but first, you need to figure out where you are on your mountain. Let's cover some important terms that you need to understand.

Capital

Here's a huge truth bomb, you will need substantial capital for real estate investing. You may not need every single penny of capital at the very beginning, but you will need sufficient capital for your first investment. After the first investment, you can save up more capital with your job income and through recycling part of your positive cash flow into your capital. There are ways to buy real estate with no money, but for the most part, it's a sucker's bet 99% of the time. You can find a few exceptions, but it's typically a mistake made by a newbie that doesn't know any better. Don't get caught up in the sales pitch. The cost of purchasing real estate without money far outweighs the pain of saving up some capital.

Credit

The same thing goes for credit. If you plan involves acquiring multiple single-family properties will require excellent credit if you want to get the best financing terms. For your first three properties, the guidelines are sometimes a little looser, so you could get by with slightly less than perfect credit. After those first three, you need a score over 720. If you're not there, then it would be a good time to look at your credit report and start taking care of the problematic accounts so that your score will go up. Any money that you put towards this is money well spent.

Financing

At this point, it's probably a good idea to talk to a lender and get preapproved. You need to figure out any possible roadblocks before you start to make a move on a property. If a lender can find those roadblocks during the preapproval process, you will be able to eliminate them now instead of them costing you money or property later.

Income

Having a strong income is the foundation that will support your chances of acquiring and financing several properties. If lending guidelines are strengthened, they will typically require the investor to qualify for the single strength of their income without counting their expected or future income. One of the biggest problems is that investors will choose to quit their job before they have finished their acquisitions, and then find that they can't finance any more properties.

Time

At first, it may seem as if time shouldn't be on this list of resources as most think they have plenty of it. But time is an important resource. The investor that can get started during their 20s has a greater advantage over people who start investing later in life. So don't brush off time.

Knowledge

Finally, when you choose to invest long-term in real estate, you need to run it just like a business. You have to make sure that you come to the table with a great amount of knowledge concerning long-term investing. There are a lot of investors who choose to defer the knowledge to an expert that they work with, and then end up getting burned. You have to know the business before you start.

Five Stages of Wealth

Using the mountain analogy from earlier, building wealth is like climbing a mountain. Most people will start at the bottom with very little, but as you make your way up the mountain, your wealth grows. The money will start to work for you instead of you trading time to earn money.

Once you reach the peak, your wealth will produce income so that you don't have to actively work for it anymore. You can still work, but you can work on your terms. You can spend time on personally rewarding activities. As you work your way up the mountain, you will go through five different stages.

1. Survival – this is where you are earning enough money to pay your bills. This also the time where you start to dig yourself out of financial holes that you dug up n the past.

2. Stability – this where you have paid off personal debts, you've built up a cash reserve, and you have built up job skills that are needed and can command a better income.

3. Saver – this when you realize your savings rate is important and you start using it. Building up wealth is pretty simple, but it's by no means easy. You have to maximize your income, decrease spending, and save money all at the same time. The best wealth builders will save 25% up to 75% of their income.

4. Growth – this where most people see investing. This is where you take your $50,000 nest egg and turn it into $1,000,000. The important things are to maximize compounding by maintaining discipline, reinvesting earnings, and buying good assets.

5. Income – this is where you have a good chunk of equity, and you are looking to enjoy the fruits of your labor. Here you need to turn equity into regular income that will provide you with flexibility and freedom.

Take a moment to look through these five things and figure out where you are currently on the mountain. Certain real estate strategies will work better for different stages. The stage doesn't have to be a perfect fit, but it's helpful to have an idea.

How Much Do You Need?

The amount of money you need to invest in real estate will depend on what you want to invest in. REITs were created in the 1960s to give regular retail investors to be a part of the commercial real estate market. These are some of the easiest and cheapest options to add real estate to a portfolio. These are traded on exchanges like stocks. Some REITs will invest in certain geographic locations or real estate area. These provide a low starting capital option. Most of these involved a starting investment of $500 to $2,500.

For people interested in physical property instead of a share of a company, private partnerships or REIGs could be for you. These give investors the chance to buy units of self-contained living space inside of a condo or apartment through an operating company. The company will manage the units, and exchange for this, they will take a percentage of the rent. Purchasing a property through a REIG will cost somewhere between $5,000 and $50,000.

Another option and one of the most popular is by becoming a landlord. With this option, you personally buy some property and rent it out. You are responsible for the mortgage, maintenance, and taxes, which means you charge enough rent to cover all these costs as well as make some. Most banks will require you to come up with at least 20% of the purchase price for a down payment. If you were interested in $100,000 property, the minimum you would need is $20,000. This amount doesn't include closing costs, which is normally around $5,000, or any other funds that you may need to get the place ready for rent.

Tip #2: Recruit a Real Estate Team

When it comes to real estate, it's like a sports team, and you are the leader. You don't technically need employees, but you will need advisors and independent contractors who can help you out in their own areas of expertise. If you don't care the idea of running a ream, then maybe you should look at another investing type.

Things can seem daunting for the person who is just starting out. However, creating an amazing team is crucial at any stage of the investing game. Your team will evolve with you. You want to make sure that you start off with the right people.

It's probably best before you start building your team that you figure out your strategy, market, and niche. It doesn't matter if you have the smartest people, if you aren't focused and clear on your strategy then there isn't a team member out there that will help.

To start, you have your inner circle. These are your closest and personal team members.

- Significant other – what you do affects them.
- Personal advisors
- Mentors – It's a good idea to try and find somebody local that is where you would like to be in five years. After you have found a mentor, figure out how you can also help them to achieve their goals. Then they will likely be willing and happy to help you with your goals.

- Business partner

Next, you have your support circle. This includes your critical or fiduciary relationships that will help you with ongoing and important tasks.

- CPA – this person plays a critical role. They should have some real estate investing knowledge. It's helpful if they understand real estate investing so that they can give you more personalized advice.

- Real estate or business attorney – you attorney should be able to help you with basic real estate knowledge. As a beginner, you need an attorney that can help you through closings and can help to review documents.

- Insurance agent – you need to find an agent that can help you. Some will insure investment properties, some don't, and some will insure flipping properties, and some don't. You need to shop around a bit as well. You may need to have more than one agent depending on the different types of properties you plan on investing in.

- Property manager – if needed. You can choose to manage a property by yourself, or you could outsource it a manager. Either way, it's a good idea to go ahead and interview some local property management companies.

- Lenders – it's best to get financing together before you need the money. You should have the terms and relationships established before you start to make offers. This way, when you start to run numbers and analyze your deals, you will know if the deal is good or if you should pass.

  o Private money lender – this is for long or short term, flexible financing

  o Hard money lender – short-term financing

  o Mortgage lender – long-term financing

Your next circle is your service circle. This is your functional relationships for the tasks that you will need after you invest.

- General contractor – this is for big remodels and pulling permits. You will have to have one if you want to flip houses unless you are a licensed general contractor. Contractors will come and go. You need to have a GC that you can trust and be good to them.

- Moisture and pest control – this is especially important if you are an owner of older rental properties. Older properties tend to have more pest problems.

- Yard service

- Painter

- Handyman – this can be tough to find a reasonably priced handyman, but if you look around, you should be able to find one. Once you find one, keep them around.

- HVAC technician

- Plumber – if you plan on owning rental properties, you need to have a reliable plumber. Find a good one you can trust, and take care of them.

- Electrician

- Home inspector

- Title company

- Closing agent

The best way for you to find all of your important team members is through networking with like-minded real estate investors. This can easily be done through REIA meetings or through business groups such as the Chamber of Commerce.

It's probably a good idea to have a talk with a realtor as well, whether you use one or not, especially if you're a beginner. Realtors can show you pretty much any house that is for sale, give you a good idea of prices, and where to find the best deals. Talk to co-workers, friends, and family for a realtor referral. It's also a good idea to talk to multiple realtors to figure out which one will work for you. You need to be upfront about your plans and goals as well. It helps if you give them something back or take them to lunch if you ask them to show you a house before you actually want to buy anything.

Tip #3: Decide on Your Investment Type

Most beginner investors know that real estate is the most popular and oldest asset classes, but what most don't realize is the number of real estate types that exist. Every type comes with its own pitfalls and benefits, which includes their own quirks in normal or appropriate standards, lending traditions, and cash flow cycles, so you need to study them before they are added to your portfolio.

The type of investor that you become will mainly be determined by the type of property you want to invest in. The top options are commercial properties, single family homes, and multi-family apartments.

As investors start to learn more about these different investment types, it is common to see someone start to build a fortune by sticking to a particular niche and specializing in it. If you truly believe real estate is where you want to devote a decent amount of resources, time, and effort in your quest for passive income and financial freedom, let's go through different types of real estate investing for you to get a decent lay of the land.

Before we get into the different investment types that you have available, I would like to take a moment to explain the reason why you should almost never buy directly in your name. There are lots of reasons, some that have to with personal asset protection. If something should go wrong, and you end up having to face something unthinkable, such as a settlement that exceeds your coverage, you will need to make sure you have the chance to place the entity that owns the real estate into bankruptcy, so that can walk away.

An important tool in making sure that your affairs are structured correctly involves choosing a legal entity. Pretty much all experienced investors use a legal structure such as a Limited Partnership or Limited Liability Company. This can save you on a lot of financial hardships that you may face. Also, hope for the best results, but plan for the worst.

These types of structures can be started with only a few hundred dollars, or if you use a decent attorney in a large city, it could be a few thousand dollars. The paperwork that is needed isn't too overwhelming, and you can choose to use a different LLC for every investment that you own. This is a technique known as asset separation because it helps to protect you and your holdings. If one of the properties ends up finding itself in trouble, you can put it into bankruptcy without hurting any of your others, as long as there was nothing signed to the contrary, like a promissory note that worked to cross-collateralized all of your liabilities.

Now we can move onto the different types of real estate.

When it comes to flipping, owning, acquiring, or developing real estate, you can get a better understanding of differences of what you are facing by splitting these real estate options into different categories.

Residential Real Estate

These are all properties that fall under the categories of vacation houses, townhouses, apartment buildings, and houses where a family or a person will pay you to live on the property. How long they stay, there will depend upon your rental agreement or lease agreement. In the US, most residential leases will last about 12 months.

Single Family Homes

These are typically the lowest risk investment option. SFR homes will typically provide you with lower monthly cash flow than other types of investment types. SFR home does provide you with a better appreciation potential

Multi-Family and Apartments

When an investor chooses multi-family units, they are typically at a greater risk of vacancies and evictions. However, any investor that is up to the challenge will be rewarded with a greater return on investment.

Commercial Real Estate

These consist of things such as skyscrapers and office buildings. If you had some money saved up, and you used it to construct a building with individual offices, you could lease those spaces out to small business owners and companies, who would then pay you rent. It's fairly common for commercial real estate to have multi-year leases. This will often prove a greater stability in your cash flow, and it can even protect the owner when the rental rates drop, but if the market were to start heating up and the rates go up substantially or a short time period, you may not be able to participate because the building is locked into an old agreement. With the potential of high holding costs and with high entry cost, commercial investments will require greater capital to maintain and invest in. They do, however, provide the investor with opportunities for appreciation and high cash-flow.

Industrial Real Estate

These properties can consist of industrial warehouses that you lease to firms as a distribution center with a long-term agreement to car washes, storage units, and other special purpose real estate that makes money from customers that temporarily use the space. Industrial real estate options will typically have service revenue streams and significant fees, like adding in coin-operated vacuum cleaners to a car wash to help up the ROI for the owners.

Retail Real Estate

These consist of strip malls, shopping malls, and any other retail stores. In some of these retail spaces, the landlord will also get a part of the sales that the stores generate, as well as the base rent as a way to incentivize them to keep the properties in perfect condition.

Mixed-Use Investments

These investment options are those that combine any of the above categories into one. One investor in California took several million dollars of his savings and located a mid-sized town in the Midwest. He then talked to a bank about financing and then build a mixed-use three-story office building that he surrounded by retail spaces. The bank that had lent him the money leased space on the ground floor and generated a decent amount of income for the owner. Other businesses, such as a health insurance company, leased out the other office spaces, and the retail spaces were quickly grabbed up by a hair salon, virtual golf range, upscale clothing store, quick service restaurant, membership gym, and Panera Bread. Mixed-use investments are popular among the investors that have a significant asset because they have a good degree of diversification, which helps to control risk.

Other Options

There are other types of ways to invest in real estate if you aren't interested in actually dealing with the properties. REITs or real estate investment trusts are popular among investors. With a REIT you buy a share of a corporation that owns properties and distributes most of its income as dividends. There are tax complexities that you have to deal with, the dividends aren't able to get the low tax rates that common stocks get, but they can be a decent addition to the right person's portfolio if you purchase them at the best valuation and with a good safety margin. You can even get into specific REIT, like hotel REITs.

There are also some esoteric areas like tax lien certificates. Lending money for real estate is technically considered to be a type of real estate investing, but it's probably more appropriate to look at it as a fixed income investment, such as a bond, because you will be generating an investment return by lending money in exchange for interest. You won't have any sort of stake in the profitability or appreciation of a property past the interest and return of the principal.

In much the same way, purchasing real estate or building, and then leasing it back to its tenant is more like fixed income investing instead of real estate investing. You are basically financing a property, although it does kind of straddle the fence between the two because, eventually, you'll get the property back and you will get the appreciation.

Your choice of investment property will determine what kind of tenants you will attract. Make sure that you completely understand the implications of your investment type. Now you need to decide how much energy and time that you are willing to put into your strategy.

Tip #4: Look at House Listings

It's important that investors understand their market. You can find pretty much every house that is for sale somewhere on the internet. It's extremely easy for investors to look houses up online and start to get an idea of what the prices are in a certain market. This is a great place to start, but eventually, you will need to see properties in person as well. You can start by driving by properties that you find interesting, and then look for open houses or talk to a realtor.

When you start to look at listings, you need to research the market forces that will impact the property to make sure that the properties you invest in don't just look good on paper. The trends of the market will vary depending on the real estate type that you choose.

- Economic indicators – some of the most important indicators for a healthy market is a low cost of living, high employment rates, and strong income growth.

- Population data – to figure out if a market is primed for investing, you should look at things like past and project job growth, migration trends, and changes in the population of surrounding cities.

- Housing data – the housing indicators for a hot market should include housing affordability, low-but-growing home prices, low vacancies, and growing average rental rates.

How to Become Financially Free

When you're looking for an investment property, you need to know the best places to look. You should look in neighborhoods or areas where at least one of the following exists: transportation, shopping, hospitals, schools, and universities. If you choose a property in a college town or a neighborhood that has a highly rated school, you have a bit of a guarantee that the tenants will probably stay long term. You will also know that demand for the property will stay high.

Having a property in these types of areas doesn't mean that you will have great tenants, but places that have these amenities usual have decent demand and good returns. Make sure you do plenty of research and ask around your chosen city or neighborhood. Driving around town looking for 'for sale' signs is a good idea.

The internet also has a wide array of online services and websites that will you in your search for an investment property. You can look at sites such as Craigslist, Zillow, Trulia, and Realtor to find properties. They provide you with lots of information on the homes that are for sale, foreclosures, and recent construction. Plus, all of the sites will give you different search options that can help you to filter your needs and requirements to help narrow down your search.

Another important part of finding properties is having a real estate network. This network should include accountants, contractors, investors, realtors, tenants, and so on. Build up this network and keep it maintained by staying in touch. If you are looking for a new property, you should be able to contact somebody in your network that knows of a good place to check out. Contacting sellers and owners directly is a good option because they could inform you of sales that have yet to be listed.

One last way to find a property is through foreclosures. When a homeowner isn't able to make their mortgage payment, the bank will repossess the property and try to resell it. This is how you can get in on foreclosures.

While it's not good that somebody has lost their home, what is great is that they are typically some of the best deals out there. Banks are typically eager to transfer the property quickly, and will give decent discounts, and will accept first offers.

Talking to local brokers and real estate agents are a great way to find foreclosures. Brokers and real estate agents work directly with banks so they should have a good bit of information about the investment. Some banks have special listing agents for foreclosures, so talk to those agents.

These are only a few ways to find the best investment properties. Locating a city where there is a decent demand for houses, use the sources on the internet, network, and look at other types of options while searching for investment properties.

Tip #5: Choose Your Investment Style

Investing styles can range from a fast turnover to full-time jobs and long-term investments to passive investments. When it comes to real estate investing, that time that you put into your investment doesn't necessarily mean you will get a better return. When you are deciding how you want to invest, make sure that you calculate the value of your time as part of the cost. These are some of the more common investment types:

- Flip and fix – this is a short-term strategy. An investor will buy a property that is need of rehab, and then they will resell the property after they have made all of the renovations. If you manage your resources and time efficiently, a flip and fix investor can make a decent amount of return on their properties.

- Owner landlord – a lot of real estate investors will choose to be a landlord, which is somebody that manages the properties that they own. The biggest benefit of being an owner landlord is that you don't have to pay a property manager. The biggest problem is that most owner landlords are inexperienced. They will typically have less experience than a property manager, which end up costing them more money and time working on their property.

- Wholesaling – a wholesaler in real estate locates investment opportunities and will then sell the contract to another investor.

Working as a middleman, the wholesaler shares the profits with investors who buy the properties. More transactions can be completed than with a traditional investor because less time is spent on the administration of deals.

- Hold and buy – this strategy in the long term. Investors will make a monthly rental income on the properties they own. As they are holding onto their properties, they hope that the value will appreciate. If done right, you could invest in properties that provide you with monthly cash flow as well as long-term appreciation.

Now, you're probably wondering if you should rent your properties or flip them since those are the most popular options when it comes to real estate investing. It really depends on you. It depends on what your goals are, so you first need to figure out your goals.

Do you want passive or active income?

Passive income is income that you can earn with very little effort. No matter what you are doing or where you are, you are still making money.

Active income will require some day to day work for you to make any money.

In the end, everybody will retire. To make sure you can do that, you have to make passive income. Active income will stop coming in when you stop working.

Flipping a house is like the day trading of real estate investing. It's not really investing, just like day trading isn't investing. But, you can still earn a lot of money from flipping, but notice how I used the word earn.

Investing is when you commit capital or money to something with the expectation of getting additional profit or income.

Speculation is when you engage in risky financial transactions with the hopes to profit from market value fluctuations of a tradable good like a financial instrument, instead of trying to profit from an underlying financial attribute in the instrument like dividends, capital gains, or interest.

You do put time and money into real estate expecting to make a profit, but a day trader also puts money into stocks and hopes to make a profit. Lots of people will put money into many different things in the hopes that they will make a profit.

The fact is, you have to put effort and time into a plan, overseeing the project, and making sure that your vision is reached within budget so that you make money once it sells. Most of the aspects are seen as active income and is considered work, not investing.

Just so you know, I'm not saying you shouldn't choose to flip houses. All I'm saying is that it should be seen more as a business and less as an investment. People can make millions by flipping houses.

When it comes to buy and hold rental properties, they are investments that are based on underlying expectations of dividends and capital gains. It's important that you can make that distinction because it will help you to figure out what you will do with your time and money.

Now, if you already have the money to retire, then take that extra cash and invest in multi-family or rental properties to make some passive income, unless you want to start a second career.

If are interested in keeping your day job, you can still get involved in real estate. If you're working full-time, then you will probably want your work in real estate to be part-time. Chances are, rental properties will probably be the easier option. They don't take as much of your time as flipping houses. With your income, you will have an easier time getting loans than if you didn't have a job, which means you can own more properties.

Now, if you don't have the money to retire, and you want to quit your job because you hate it, then you should try your hand at rental properties and house flipping. The income you make by flipping will help to replace your salary. The rental properties will help you prepare for retirement. You first need to make sure that you are financially ready to quit your job and invest in real estate before you actually do it.

Tip #6: Start Raising Cash for Your Reserves and Down Payment

Most new real estate investors don't know how much money they need to have reserved when they start out in the real estate business.

Most education programs focus on learning how to buy with no money down and no credit. This is perfectly doable, but all investors will need cash at some point. The big question is how much is needed.

What most want to know is how much money banks and lenders require an investor to have to able to qualify for a mortgage. This will vary between the different loan programs and lenders. Some may not require any assets while others will require six months reserves for the property.

This might not be too bad for some investing pros since it is not likely that a property will go unrented for six months. There are some situations that could come up like a delay in flipping a house, tenants that are renting to own, and the condition of the property that might cause you to spend some extra cash to cover costs.

Investors that buy and hold properties must rely on their education to help when figuring out how much of a reserve you need to replace broken appliances, normal maintenance, and any quick fixes between tenants. These costs are normal and need to be budgeted for.

It is perfectly normal to have to use financing when buying real estate and there are many options for you to choose from. Here are some financing sources to choose from:

- FHA Loans: These are insured by the government, and it is fairly easy to qualify for these programs. The terms might include a long-term loan, fixed interest rate, and a small down payment.

- VA Loans: To qualify for these you need to be a veteran. The terms might include a long-term loan, fixed interest rate, and zero down.

- Conforming Loans: These loans conform to guidelines from the mortgage giants like Freddie Mac and Fannie Mae. The terms might include a long-term loan, fixed interest rate, and require 5 to 20 percent down.

- Portfolio Loans: These are held by lending institutions or banks instead of being sold on the mortgage market. The terms will vary but will have competitive interest rates and shorter terms like five to ten years.

- Hard Money Loans: All these lenders are interested in is the collateral instead of the regulations. The costs are higher and are usually used for remodeling projects.

- Private Lenders: Private lenders will vary greatly. They could be wealthy individuals, or self-directed 401ks and IRAs. The long-term relationship and flexibility you receive from these lenders make them very valuable.

- Seller Financing: This is the best type of financing. If a seller has equity, they could let you pay the purchase price with installments over time or use contracts and leases. It isn't easy to find a seller who is willing to finance. The flexibility of the terms makes seller financing worth it.

The financing you decide to use will depend on your situation, personal preference, and strategy. You need to rely on your team members and mentors to help you find the best for you.

When you have figured out your financing plans, you can move on to raising the cash for reserves and down payments.

Investing in real estate allows you to use money from others to get you moving forward. You don't need to try to build your business with no money down. You still need money for reserves.

The amount you will need depends on your property criteria, the prices in your market, and your strategy. You can ask your lender how much you will need for a down payment or certain loan programs.

You want to use a strategy of house hacking to buy a duplex for $125,000. You find an FHA loan that requires 3.5 percent down. This will run you $4,375. You will probably need about $3,000 for closing costs. You might need even more if the property needs some improvements. Remember those rainy day reserves, too. Let's estimate another $10,000.

The total cash you will need for this extremely low down payment scenario will be $17,375. How can you find this money? Here are some ideas:

- Save: Yes, this one is very obvious. You need to make investing the most important part of your life. Make some extra income, cut out unnecessary expenses and just be patient until you get the money you need. No shortcuts here, but it will work with time.

- Sell: It sounds drastic but sell your car and get a cheaper one. If you have expensive toys, sell these until you can afford to get them later on. Sell a property that has plenty of equity if you can downsize. If you have a garage, basement, or attic full of collectibles, try selling these to help you raise some money.

- Borrow: You have to be careful if you decide to do this. Lines of credit, credit cards, and personal loans that get used for down payments are dangerous if they make a turn for the worse. The main problem is the discipline in cash flow. Whatever the amount you need to borrow, you must make sure the investment will produce enough money to pay the interest. If it doesn't, that money has to come out of your pocket. You need to be certain you can make an extra loan payment if the worst case scenario were to happen.

- Partner: Finding a partner is like sharing a cake. If somebody offered you a triple layered chocolate cake for half off, but you didn't have enough money to buy it. It makes sense to ask a friend to buy the cake, and you share it. It is a win-win for both. This is the awesomeness of partnering. It will work as long as you communicate well and work with people you trust and like.

There will always be unexpected expenses. You need to stash away a large reserve that will help you with any possible hazards. The need for a large amount of cash could be minimized by having plans to help with emergencies. These could include business, the person, and property insurance and having tools on hand to fix minor repairs yourself.

It might not be covered in all real estate programs this money is what you need in addition to paying yourself. You should take a percentage of each payday and set this aside for any business or personal emergencies that could arise.

Tip #7: Locate Real Estate Deals

Real estate is attracting investors once again. It is a great way to build wealth, and it's great to see people wanting to put their financial future in good hands. It can also be a problem.

The more people are trying to buy real estate; it will be harder to find deals. It is a simple case of supply and demand.

The way investors in that past found deals is changing quickly. Savvy investors are changing how they find deals. If you want what nobody else can get, then you will have to do what nobody wants to do to get it.

Deals are not going to land in your lap. Finding the right deals is like hunting for treasure. You must turn over dozens of stones before you find the gem.

During times of recession, deals are very easy to find. To quote Warren Buffett as he described the years between 2008 and 2011, "Every decade or so, dark clouds will fill the economic skies, and they will briefly rain gold. When downpours of that sort occur, it's imperative that we rush outdoors carrying washtubs, not teaspoons."

We always need to carry our washtubs, so we are ready for this rain. During normal economic times, you will have to work hard and make a plan to bring these deals to you. You must remain disciplined with your investment, so you don't get caught up in the fever of the market.

You need to create a plan to help you find deals. The first needs to be a budget for marketing. If you don't have any money for marketing, you have to be creative and plan to give up personal time. It is more challenging but not impossible. If you have about $500 a month, you could create some workable marketing. If you have $1,000, you could set yourself up in the market. Investing in marketing will always be your best return for your money. You must choose carefully to find the right campaigns.

There are several campaigns to choose from. Since it is not an exact science, these campaigns could change just like the wind. Test the different campaigns carefully and find what works.

Here are some of the best campaigns organized from least to most expensive:

- Multiple Listing Service Campaign: Locate a buyer's agent that is willing to send you leads. These agents can set up emails that will automatically go to your inbox each time a new property hits to market. You have to move fast with these deals. We are talking minutes now hours here. Other people are using this same campaign.

- Flyers: Create postcard sized flyers or cards with messages and place them on cars. Do this as often as you can. Walk around shopping malls, hospitals, parking garages, etc. and place the flyers on the cars. Check with local laws to make sure you aren't doing anything illegal. Once people begin to call, make sure to take their information, find out what they are looking for, ask questions and listen to them. Keep the information organized so you can go back to it when needed.

- Networking and Referral Campaign: Tell everybody to send you leads. Talk to family and friends. Reach out to property managers, real estate agents, financial advisers, attorneys, or your CPA. Go to meeting at REIAs, landlord associations, and other business-related meetups. Have business cards and flyers printed up with your criteria so people can remember you.

- Walk or Drive: Regularly drive or walk to the neighborhood of your choice. Look for vacant properties without signs, run-down properties that have been listed with agents, For Rent signs, and For Sale By Owner signs. Call the numbers listed on signs and talk to the agents or owners if at all possible. For properties without signs, talk to neighbors to see if they know who owns the property. Write down the addresses and look up the information at your convenience. You can find the address from the local tax assessor's office. You can find possible phone numbers with the whitepages.com or other online phone listings. You could either send them a letter or call them and ask them about the house.

- Locate Wholesalers: Some people find deals for investors. Wholesales usually control deals and quickly sell them for a bit more to investors. Talk to them, ask to be put on their mailing lists and be proactive.

- Bird Dogs: Bird dogs will send you leads. You will follow up on the leads and turn them into a deal. The bird dog will need to have a real estate license for you to legally pay a finder's fee.

- Cold Calls: If you can handle being rejected 50 times for each promising call, this is an effective method. You can look online in the classifieds to find rent by owner or for sale by owner listings. Just call these and ask questions. Not many people can do this, so you might find gems that others are passing up.

- Classified Ads: You could choose to advertise your service through free classified ads either in local publications or online. Not all avenues will work, but if they are free or low cost, try as many as you can to get your info out there.

- Direct Mail: Send out postcards and letters to different property owners. Finding a list is as simple as paying a list company. Sometimes it is a wild goose chase. Don't get discouraged. Just remember to follow up with them. Here are a few lists that work well:

  o Absentee owners or houses that are not occupied by the actual owners.

- o Long-time homeowners or houses that are occupied by the owners.

- o Owners who have many units.

- o Landlords who have recently evicted a tenant.

- o Owners whose listing has expired recently.

- o Owners who have delinquent property taxes.

- o Probate and estate properties.

- o Properties are getting ready to be foreclosed on.

- Social Media and websites: Social media and websites and just like online business cards that will let people know about your investing business. It will let people know who you are, what you want, and how you could help them. Make it easy for people to get in touch with you.

- BiggerPockets Marketplace: Each day, listings are posted, and real transactions are taking place because of these listings. You can post ads for either something you are trying to sell or something you are looking for. If you are looking for certain properties, make a post. Looking to sell a property, make a post. Want to find a partner, make a post. Make sure you use the Keyword Alert System when you make your post, so you get notified every time that word is used. Remember to put your city into your ad.

- Craigslist: Craigslist is an online classified that is free to use. It is a good source to find real estate deals. There are three things to do on Craigslist:

  - Search for Sellers: The easiest way to use Craigslist is just to search for real estate postings. You can do this easy and can have new leads sent to your inbox. The only problem with this is there are many people already using this.

  - Post Ads: Don't wait for the deals to come to you. Post an ad to tell people what you are looking for. Make it flashy and bid. You need to get people's attention.

  - Look for Landlords: Get in touch with landlords that are posting on Craigslist. When you call them to let them know you are looking to invest in real estate and that you do not want to rent. You want to buy their property. If they don't want to sell that particular property, they might have one they want to sell or know someone else who wants to sell.

- Car Signs: Use vinyl or magnetic lettering on your car to let people know you buy houses. I can simply say "I Buy Houses" and has a contact number. This might be out of your comfort zone, but it is inexpensive.

- Yard Signs: When you are trying to rent or sell a house, put an "I Buy Houses" sign beside your for rent sign if the local law allows it. Signs are a good way to generate leads.

- Advertising: Use ads like radio advertising, community bulletins, magazines, newspapers, and online in Google Adwords. This cost could get out of hand, but if you are careful, it could be a good return on investment.

Decide on whether you want to do a marketing or budget campaign. More campaigns could be shared here, but these are the best options, to begin with. Figure out a budget and chose a couple of campaigns, to begin with.

Whatever you decide, be passionate about it. You will be amazed at how many people actually want you to achieve your goals and are willing to help you out. Tell everyone you know about what you are doing. Who knows, the person you are talking to might just have a property they are looking to sell.

As the real estate industry continues to grow you have two choices, you can sit it out and wait for the next crash, or you can do what you need to and find the next big deal. Get out there and find that one deal that will set you apart from the others.

Tip #8: Learn How to Negotiate

Most people don't realize they can open up negotiations by offering the seller one dollar. Yes, you read that right. One dollar. You probably won't get the property for one dollar, but it is a great icebreaker. Your negotiation skills will improve with experience.

Some are afraid of negotiating. You don't have to be. They are just a conversation. If you truly think about it, you negotiate every day of your life. You negotiate with co-workers, salespeople, friends, spouse, and children. You aren't afraid of those conversations. Absolutely not. Why are you afraid of conversations that deal with finances?

There is an old saying that, "everything in real estate is negotiable." This is very true. You can negotiate what furniture stays with the property, the amount of the rent, the payment period, payment conditions, and price of the property.

Negotiation is important when purchasing a rental property since it is the best way to get a great deal. New investors will lack good negotiation skills. Experienced, successful investors are professionals when it comes to negotiating a deal.

Here are some tips to help you negotiate your next investment property:

- Check Your Finances: Real estate investing deals with how much you can invest to make you money. Before you start negotiating, you need to check your finances. Find out how much cash you have and what options you have available to you. Make a budget to see

39

what you can spend on a rental property. Think about recurrent expenses and one-time costs. What you have on hand and what you might make in rental income. You need to aim to have positive cash flow from the very beginning. You can't buy a rental property if it is too expensive for your budget to handle. You can't risk having a negative cash flow. After you have looked at your finances, you will know what you can afford to spend on a rental property. When you enter negotiations, stick to this price since it determines your profits.

- Perform a Market Analysis: After you have found a property you are interested in, do a comparative real estate market analysis to get all the comparisons for the purchase. Figure out what similar properties in the area are being sold for in the prior weeks and months. Find out what they sold for instead of asking about the prices since these will be giving you better prices on what your rental would be worth. Finding an investment property calculator could help since it shows you prices for thousands of properties in the United States. It will also show you the number of bathrooms, bedrooms and square footage. When you have done your market analysis, you will have a better idea of what price you should try to buy the property for during negotiations.

- Identify the Market: To be successful during negotiations, you should know which market you will be negotiating in a seller's market or buyer's market. Some of the common indicators like trends in the closing percentages, house prices, selling versus listing prices, time property stays on the market, and how many houses are listed. These will help you decide if you should purchase a property in a seller's or buyer's market. Buying in a buyer's market is different from buying in a seller's market. With a buyer's market, you can take time before you close the deal, you have time to make a lower offer, ask for better terms like asking for repairs to be done or leaving some appliances. In a seller's market, you must act fast. You will pay a higher price, to offer better conditions, and don't expect anything to come with the property. The competition is strong, and you aren't going to have any bargaining powers when negotiating.

- Hire an Agent: Real estate agents do cost you money, but they could get you a better deal than you could do by yourself. This will hold true for rental investors. More experienced ones will be able to make a deal by themselves. Your agent will be speaking to the seller's agent instead of you talking to the seller. This is how investing works.

- Know Why the Seller is Selling: Before you begin negotiations, you need to figure out why the seller is selling. Knowing will give you more leverage during the negotiations.

You will know when you can press harder and when you just need to give up.

- Negotiate Everything: When you have decided to buy a property, you have to negotiate everything, not just the price. Negotiate the appliances, furniture, repairs, appraisal contingency, home warranty, financing contingencies, closing date, and closing costs. All aspects of real estate are negotiable. You might not get the price you want if it's in a seller's market and you can't do anything about it. You could get a better deal by getting other benefits instead of just those listed above. These might add up some value to your profits and rental properties.

- Be Reasonable: Never try to get more out of the seller that you reasonably expect. If a single-family property that has not furniture, fireplace, or pool but sold for $500,000 in the same neighborhood a few weeks ago, don't try to get yours that has furniture, fireplace, and a pool for less than this. It doesn't matter how much you like the property, don't pay more than what you can afford. You are buying an investment, not your own dwelling. It is a pure business transaction. During negotiations, make just the decisions that make sense for an investor.

- Compromise: You have to be willing to make compromises during a seller's market. Make these offers in the form of compensation to the seller. They will more likely bring down the price. Don't compromise what you can't afford like accepting a price higher than your budget. You need to compromise reasonably.

Purchasing an investment property is the best way to expand your investment business or the first step in becoming an investor. You need to do whatever you can to get the best deal. Use the tips above to help you negotiate the best price and terms for purchasing your next income property.

Tip #9: Make Your First Investment

Investment property is a great way to begin a real estate portfolio and get started in the rental game. It is easy to get excited when you make your first buy, but you need to take it slow and proceed with caution. Jumping in too soon might be costly for buyers. It is a hard lesson to learn. You might wind up with an investment that will cost you more than what you originally thought.

If you can take these tips to heart, you might avoid some common problems when buying your first property:

- Don't Be Eager: When you start looking for your very first property, don't ever chase a deal. Many first time investors will overpay because they want to get started and are too excited. Know your numbers and don't exceed the correct price during an auction or if you are negotiating with the owner of the property.

- Spend Some Time There: Sit at the property during the hours of 6 am, and 9 am and again from 9 pm to midnight before you ever decide to buy. By sitting in your car, you can see what is happening around the neighborhood and building during these times.

- Check Its Value: If you can buy a property below County Appraisal District, you have just hit a home run. Other factors need to be considered too like updates, repairs, etc.

- Use Your Head Instead of Your Heart: Being a first-time investor means you won't always have the luxury of buying using your gut feeling. You will need to buy using a large margin to take into account what you don't know, what you do know and everything beyond and above that. Purchasing rental properties can get expensive. Just a couple of bad decisions could take you completely out of the game. Buy only if the numbers make complete sense to you.

- Location: Remember the old adage: location, location, location. If you can find a property that can carry itself like the rental payments easily covers the maintenance, insurance, taxes, and gives you some cash flows, the appreciation will give you the opportunity to refinance for higher rental incomes and if you decide to sell, a larger sale price.

- Know Your Numbers: Many new investors will buy a flip deal without leaving any room for error. In a hot market, real estate brokers, agents, and wholesalers will sell you deals that will not make any sense. Try to find flips where your costs are less than 68 percent of the fair market value. You would have the best chance of having a clean exit if the market were to correct.

- Be Patient: When purchasing real estate, if prices do fall, it doesn't mean you will lose money on your investment. Real estate is a recurring industry. You do have an asset that backs up your investment. If you need an exit strategy, you can either refinance or rent instead of just selling. With time, prices will rebound. Just be patient.

- Choose a Buddy: Find someone to go in with on your first investment. Get advice from a professional to make sure you aren't missing anything that could cost you money in the long run. Team up with someone you trust who has the experience to help you with your first few purchases.

- Go For It: There are so many people who constantly say, "I wish I knew how to get into real estate investing." Having rental properties is very profitable. Choose the right location to find the best tourist market. Know your local rates on long-term rentals. Know the rates on short-term rentals. Know how to leverage your intel for funds.

- Decide on Passive or Active Investing: Active investing is hard and time-consuming. It is also hard to become successful if it is not your only job. Many first time buyers don't have the experience, tools, or time to stay away from problems. Building up your experience with passive investing is a great way to begin. Once you have learned more, you can reevaluate if being active is the right way to go.

Your ultimate goal is building wealth. How you invest will change as you become more experienced as an investor. The main thing is to keep your goals in mind. Keep on course and make the right choices. Soon you will be enjoying significant financial returns when investing in real estate.

The ultimate investment is a turnkey investment. This lets you buy a renovated rental that already has a tenant in place. This tenant gives you a monthly cash flow with their rental payments. The house will appreciate with time. Real estate investors have found success with passive income turnkey investments.

When you have successfully paid off all your properties, take a victory lap and enjoy the fruits of your labor. You have earned it. You set your goals that looked like they were going to be unattainable. You created a plan and executed it. You can now reap the rewards. You can do what you want.

You could also look at a bigger capital base and figure out if you would like to explore options your capital offers. Strategies and assets that were out of your reach when you began are now within reach. If something looks good, you could exit/exchange some or all of your assets to buy another property.

Tip #10: Prioritize Your Next Steps

For many real estate investors being able to prioritize their tasks is an exhausting and daunting challenge. It is easy to spend hours and hours going from one activity to another without accomplishing a thing. By the end of a week or possibly a month, you are wondering what happened to time and where you will find your next sale. An obvious solution is learning to prioritize the things that are important to you and what has the largest impact on your life. If you can learn to focus on what is important, you will become a lot more productive.

You must be realistic. If real estate investing is the most important thing in your life, you need to be ruthless about your priorities. This is not going to be a forever project. You will spend the most time in the first few months of getting your business started. Later on, as you have bought some properties and gained some momentum, you will spend less time on the business.

All the things you do during the day can either help you or sends you back a step. There is a difference between doing what will have long-term effects on your business like networking and meetings along with doing tasks that have immediate impacts. You must have a steady stream of leads constantly coming in like closing deals and making offers. You need to do things that will impact these areas.

How much time can you invest? You need to spend no less than ten hours each week to give yourself a chance at success. The more time you can spend, for instance, 20 to 30 hours, your chances will increase.

Take a look at your calendar and pick certain times to spend on your business every week. If your plans include a real estate deal on Saturday morning, mark it on your calendar so nothing else will get in the way. This is just like keeping a doctor or dentist appointment. It has to be scheduled for you to make it a priority. After you have blocked off this time, you will be able to focus on the actions you need to take during this time.

When you begin to break down the sections in your business cycle, figure out what you have to do to have success in these areas. You might fool yourself into thinking you are working since you have been accomplishing little tasks. This won't make it true. Even though you are caught up in your mailings or evaluating deals doesn't necessarily mean you are hard at work.

When you have scheduled your time, it is now time for action. This simply means you should spend time doing the actions that will move you toward your goals. If you need to, break large projects or goals into small actions that can be accomplished easily and mark them off your list.

Break it down into these simple steps:

1. Find Your Next Project: Write down a couple of projects that you have to do NEXT to begin a real estate deal. Projects can be anything that takes more than one step to finish.

2. Find Your Next Action: Write down the next several actions you need to do for your

projects to move forward. Put these in your time slot you have scheduled for real estate investing.

3. Do Your Next Action: Sounds simple, right? Just do what you have written down in the next time slot.

4. Find Your Next Action, Again: This process will continue to repeat itself. You will continue to find more actions until every project is done.

What will happen when you have finished all the projects? You have finished your goal. Then make a new goal and move on to accomplishing it.

You should be moving in and out of tasks at lightning speed with all the resources and technology at your fingertips. There are various ways you can outsource all your busywork to virtual assistants. You should focus on what is important and the things that will benefit your business the best. If your best strength is networking, you need to meet with at least one new contact each week. If you can do this for six weeks, you will begin to see benefits that can help your business grow. Business cards and a website is important, but don't spend an entire day on them.

It can be easy to forget you are trying to build a business when you get caught up in the day to day world. If it was simple, everybody would have a successful investing business. This is a difficult business and takes hard work. Having good time management skills are a hidden strength that many investors possess. They know what to outsource and who they can outsource to. They know what they can successfully do and when the right time is to do it. If you can focus on how you run your business, you can help your process and the things you do each day.

You only have a certain amount of hours every day. You need to use them productively. If you can remember this each day and stay focused on what makes a difference, your business will bloom, and you will see bigger benefits.

Common Mistakes to Avoid

The number of success stories along with the chance for great returns make real estate investing tantalizing, but taking that leap into investing in real estate need not be taken lightly. People are looking to break into real estate investing need to conduct large amounts of research before they get started so that they can avoid rookie mistakes.

While you can't deny that experience is the perfect way to learn, you can use a lot of resources to help you avoid some of the more common mistakes. Let's take a look five of the most common real estate investing mistakes that are often made by new investors, and how you can avoid them.

Allowing Yourself to Be Limited to a Certain Market

When you reach the time to choose where you want to invest, your home market will probably feel the safest since you are familiar with it, but that doesn't mean it's your best choice. There are no borders when it comes to opportunity, and that needs always to be a consideration as you start to look for an investment.

Here's an example: It's hard for people that live in a large metro area like Los Angeles or New York to locate long-term rental properties in their immediate area that will give them strong yields, let alone the price. There are lots of other markets across the US that provide high returns, a strong need for housing, and economic stability, so why pigeonhole yourself in those metro areas?

Advances in services, technology, and data have played a crucial role in development by allowing investors to research and find markets all over the nation as they look at better opportunities. By access, these services will give the investors clarity and transparency for opportunities outside of their home markets. This will empower them to find top-performing investment markets and know that they are secure in their decisions.

Under- or Over-renovating

Knowing the number of renovations a property will need is key to making a successful deal. An investor needs to aim to renovate to local market level and realize that renovations will change depending on the neighborhood, even within the same city.

Regardless of the property's condition, knowing the scope of rehab is an analysis that will require lots of focus. Investors will often find themselves in a sticky situation if they renovate a property beyond the market. If all of the homes within a neighborhood has tile countertops, and you choose to make yours granite, it probably won't be a worthy investment because it doesn't cater to the typical owner or renter within that area. This may limit your ROI by creating only a marginal impact on the sales price or rental rate.

You can avoid under- or over-renovating by talking to local professionals. They are market experts that may be able to help you decide on which improvements would be worthy. It's also a good idea to tour other houses in your area or look at online resources to get a feel for the competition.

Not Understanding Debt

There are two main reasons that real estate investors will get debt:

1. To improve their buying power. Instead of spending $100,000 of equity on one property, financing will allow that money to go further by letting the investor to spread it out over several properties with less of a down payment on each property.

2. To improve returns. When an investor can get a debt with a lower interest rate than the net yield of investment, the ROI is higher than if they used cash.

Both of these options may look good, but getting debt doesn't come without some risks, which is where beginners need to be careful. The less experienced investor could take on a lot of debt that has a higher interest rate than investment yields. You will then suffer from negative cash flow. You will then have to take money out of pocket to cover the shortfall so that you can avoid defaulting.

To avoid this, you need to crunch the numbers of a deal so that you know that a property will provide you the revenues to cover the loan.

Doing Everything by Yourself

A lot of investors will take on their first couple of deals part-time while still working in their primary profession without any help. With inexperience and lack of time, it's not that surprising that a lot of people will fail.

It can be challenging to stay on top of everything that is involved in real estate investing when you have a full-time profession. If you start investing without focus or resources, you may put a good deal in a bad position. Before you get started, you need to have a clear scope of your work and a good understanding of how all of this works. You also need other people to help you out when you can't do something yourself.

Not Having Money for Maintenance and Repairs

The last mistake that new investors will make is not setting realistic expectations when it comes to capital expenditures and maintenance costs. The best investors will set aside 2% of the property value into a reserve each year for any potential costs.

Novices normally don't set anything aside and find their self it a tough spot when a repair is needed because they don't have the capital. Everything that makes up your investment has its own lifespan and will eventually have to be replaced.

Conclusion

Thank you for making it through to the end of *10 Real Estate Investing Tips from Experts*. Let's hope it was informative and able to provide you with all of the tools you need to achieve your goals.

The next step is to make use of these ten tips. Whether you have already dabbled in real estate investing, or you're a complete beginner, start with tip number one, and make your steps towards real estate success. Success will take some time, but if you don't do things smartly, and don't get ahead of yourself, you are sure to see your investments pay off.

Finally, if you found this book useful in any way, a review on Amazon is always appreciated!

Description

Real estate investing is one of the more popular forms of investing. It doesn't seem as scary as the stock market, and you do, to an extent, have more control over it. If done the right way, it can lead to financial freedom. Anybody can be successful in real estate investing if they follow a plan and take steps towards minimizing losses.

This book is here to help you do just that. Throughout these pages, you will find ten investing tips that will help you reach a life of financial freedom. In this book you will learn:

- The importance of a good team
- The different types of investment styles and types
- How to find the best deals
- How to negotiate
- And much more

Real estate is a great opportunity to make active and passive income. If you follow these ten tips, you will see lots of success in the real estate world. That's not to say these ten tips are the only tips you need, but they are definitely a great place to start. Get this book today, and be well on your way to financial freedom.